MW01537011

DREAM JOURNAL

THIS JOURNAL BELONGS TO :

....

Made in the USA
Coppell, TX
29 September 2022

83804621R00063